Thoughts

of a

Gentleman

Works by Terry Gingles

Thoughts of a Gentleman: Works of Terry Gingles

Copyright © 2015 by Terry Gingles

Editing by Randall Croom

Cover Design by Michael Velasquez

ISBN: 978-0-692-43482-6

Published in the United States of America 2015 by

Artist by the Sea Productions
TerryGingles@gmail.com
Twitter: @terrygingles

For Terry Sr. and Mildred Gingles

Thank you for everything

Contents

Introduction I

"If anything, do it for your Mom and Dad." It was those nine words uttered by my good friend Shay Roundtree on a cool November evening in Los Angeles at our favorite watering hole that motivated me to put this book together. Prior to that conversation I had toyed around with the idea of publishing my poems but never was very serious about executing a plan of completion. At that moment in the bar it finally made sense to follow through and take this journey. The reward of handing my parents a book of completed works published by their son put an instant smile on my face. Finally, something they can hold to justify this long artistic journey I have been on.

I have been writing poetry for fifteen years now and it wasn't doing anything but taking up valuable space on my hard drive. Writing is a way I release stress, so I was only writing these for myself as a way to get by. After you write at least five poems a week for fifteen years one can put together a decent size collection. I decided in this book to only published poems I wrote from 2012 through early 2015. I may at a later date release some of my earlier work because through this journey I was able to revisit those words too, and I found them pretty damn interesting.

Though these poems are not presented in the chronological order that they were created, there is indeed an order to the chaos. I found the task of putting together this book a difficult one. As I stated earlier, I wrote these for myself so I was not holding anything back. Once this book is published I will feel naked to the world because it is 100% me in these words. At times I felt the need to rewrite a poem or two just

Terry Gingles

because my initial reaction was that I was revealing a lot of myself. After careful thought, I decided not to because someone may read this, recognize a situation I was in, see they're not alone and that there is light at the end of the tunnel.

So with that being said enjoy Thoughts of a Gentleman: Volume One!

Terry Gingles

Los Angeles, California

March 19th 2015

Introduction II

On April 8, 2015, as I sat at my computer putting the finishing touches on this book the story of Walter Scott broke in the media. Walter Scott, a 50 year old Black Man was shot in the back and killed by a police officer in South Carolina. I was forced to watch the video over and over because apparently it is okay for the media to broadcast an actual murder on television these days. Each replay taking its toll on my heart and soul, I became speechless. I wanted to tweet or post a status update to show my anger and pain but couldn't. I was left with no other choice but to do what I do best and that was to write.

Terry Gingles

This Here Fruit

That strange fruit ain't so strange no more

As dark ripe fruit slowly hits the floor

The harvest in America is at an overabundance

Proudly leading the world in this here mass production

"The tree stole water and resources from earth"

That ole media spin causing the fruit to lose worth

"It was hanging too low, which caused this lump on my head

I had to pick him off or I could end up dead"

Excuses like that of course we'll hear

But when you examine those words they're draped in fear

From a coward suited up in a badge and boots

Scared of the nutrients and resolve in this here fruit

God help us

THOUGHTS OF A GENTLEMAN

Terry Gingles

Lost Souls

We're all lost souls.

Some seem to wear bandages,

While others can't seem to manage it,

Displaying our open wounds so others can judge and slander it.

Feel better now?

Of course you're better than me.

How silly was I to wear a broken heart on my sleeve.

Fuck off!

On The Rocks

She knows my wounds run deep

Yet she continues to give

Give give give

She never takes

I'd like to think of her as reliable

Old faithful

Always on time

Her selflessness gives me a warm feeling inside

Never does she not step up to the plate

I've had others but none like her

You'd think with as much love she gives I'd want to stay

But I know this can't last forever

Though I wish it could

She's mused so many of what I'd like to think are my greatest ideas

I don't know

Maybe I would have come up with them without her being around

I mean I do fancy myself as a creative guy

With that being said

Until that day I build up the courage to leave

Can I have one more kiss from your cold lips please

Terry Gingles

Loosies and Cigarillos

Loosies and cigarillos. Costing lives of Negroes.

2014, and that bird still crows.

Jim is his name, smiling with no shame.

Their sights steady aim, yet find a way to blame

Their actions on us, fuck some evidence.

Got us looking around asking, "Is it really just us?"

Can't wear a hood, can't use my pockets,

can't drive a car, police ready to stop it.

Choirboy, I gotta be, you call me a boy before you murder me

then call me a race-baiter when I question the perjury.

#Blacklivesmatter? Shit, that's just chatter.

Let another Ebola come around and next week it won't matter.

The latest hashtag while news reporters brag

about the new followers gained, that they never had.

Next week a new ass will break the internet, soon forgetting the innocent,

on to the next topic for relevance.

But me, I'm not allowed to live and let be

when I'm haunted by my brother screaming, "I can't breathe."

Because that could be any one of us, when a cop doesn't trust,

shitting his pants and scared while trying to get me to hush

It's not resisting when I'm fighting for my life!

I'm not insane when I feel something's not right!

I'm running low on energy to continue this fight.

Calling for my guardian angels to please take flight.

Wrap your wings around me, protect me from the police

who seem to have a problem with me being me.

Roses + Concrete

Look at all those roses growing from the concrete.

Different colors too, looking lush and beautiful.

Now they try everything they can to put a stop to this.

In their eyes the roses are labeled an eye sore.

So they spray pesticides, lay down new layers of concrete or go for the quick kill, pull them by the stem and yank them from the ground.

They'll pour tons of resources into figuring out a solution to get rid of these damn dirty roses.

Not knowing those rose's roots run deep and are one with the earth.

That's why them roses keep sprouting and can't be contained.

They were hand planted by God and grow towards his sun.

The rest of planet took notice and now they all want one.

A rose garden that is, they connect with its beauty.

Despite the thorns and scratches on the petals, they love the relaxing smell that they give.

There's one more thing that those roses tend to offer freely,

Their breath, which is the oxygen we breathe.

Without it man couldn't exist.

Without it, they wouldn't exist.

Maybe that's why they're mad!

Something they deem so worthless provides the air that they need.

Perhaps they're jealous that they themselves weren't roses.

We'll never know, but I do know this.

Jealously leads to anger and anger leads to hate and hate leads to suffering.

And only a person suffering from a lack of self-love can utter the words,

"Fuck your breath"

Terry Gingles

No, Not Now

"No, not now," I say real low

"No, not now," my volume begins to grow

Having the best day ever and then you pop by

No knock at the door, not even saying hi

I thought if I left you, you'd be gone for good

I look over my shoulder and there you stood

You chuckle and smirk as you puff on a square

You look right through me as though I'm not even there

I glance at my chest to see what you see

A glimmer of hope with freshly blooming leaves

I shake my head no and place my hands on my heart

"You can't have it this time, I'll tear you apart."

You raise your eyebrows and cock your head to the side

Those piercing dark pupils stared deep in my eyes

"Perhaps another time, you're on to my ploy

You'll be back soon enough, you pathetic, depressed boy."

Strawberry Scented Lotion
and Powdered Sugar Necks
(For Roxie)

Grace and elegance sway from each step

Hips that bare mankind move from right to left

Their soft skin vibrates my heart with each touch

Energy so irresistible, it overspills my cup

The essence of their smell, the flow of their hair

Are just two things that ignite the intensity of my stare

A creature that's more precious than the diamonds on earth

It's truly a blessing when one truly understands their worth

That extra pep in their step when their mane is set

Their perfect round belly buttons that glisten when wet

Delicate looking feet, the foundation of their strength

The long sturdy legs that seem to get sexier with length

There are little things they do, they're hard to resist

Like when they powder their noses or pucker their lips

Nothing better than to laying your eyes on one's bare silhouette

Not too many things I'd call flawless but you embody perfect

So here's my tip of the hat to the opposite sex

With their Strawberry scented lotion and powdered sugar necks

Terry Gingles

Can I Live

Not round enough for the circles, not square enough for the squares.

Objectified from all angles, shyly embracing their stares.

That's how life can be when you split the fence.

Pulled from both sides, as you grunt and wince.

But what both sides don't know you embrace them both.

"Can I just be me?" One can only hope.

It's not my fault that I like this, and sometimes I like that,

Sometimes I wear white, other times I wear black.

But I'm just me, at the core I'm human.

When said out loud I can see you fuming.

But just chill out, everything's just fine

You should live your life, 'cause I'm gonna live mine.

And when it's all said and done, while you're checking my list,

You'll look back and be mad at the life you missed.

Can I live?

My Own Road

She stands in the middle of the road

Cause that's the only place she fits

She doesn't know how to go north or south

East or west

Fast or slow

She stands

Alone

You think she's crazy

Which is why she's cool when you pass her by

I think she's amazing

And love that she sticks out

So I stopped as the other cars behind me began to honk

I didn't give a damn

I mean look at her

Beautiful, brave and independent

I let down my window and took a moment as I took her in

Her long locs blew in the wind

Her face seemed to be stuck with a permanent grin

Terry Gingles

I told her "I'd offer you a ride but I don't think you need one"

She slowly shook her had no

as the flower in her hair was struck by a breeze

my natural reaction was to smile

I recognized that special place she was in

I hadn't touched that in a while

So best believe I wasn't going to disturb her's

My foot massaged the gas as I decided to move on

But I kept my eyes on my rearview as I pushed up that road

Her image grew smaller

Smaller

Smaller

And smaller

Until she was no longer there

But little does she know

She inspired me

She inspired me to go out and find my own road

Find my own place

Find my own peace

And you know what

That's exactly what I did

Chasing The Dragon

My eyes smiled once they connected with you.

My heart blushed once it thought of you.

The speed of sound slowed down to a graceful pace,

And with eyes closed I used the word love to describe this taste

So fulfilling, so rich, so sweet

No longer do I travel the world to seek

My better half, in you, I'm home

Two sparrows in our tree singing our song

Nothing, or no one never seems to matter

They can hear the bond through our synched and jolly laughter

Nothing is more potent, you're the high I seek

Chasing the dragon daily because of you I'm complete

Light Years Apart

Even the brightest stars that appear next to each other are still light years apart.

And so goes the love I have for you, where it began, I can't start

Was it when I looked into your eyes and I didn't sigh

At the loneliness that you held, very deep inside

Or was it the light that shined when you opened up the truth

That was deep inside of you even past the root

Kindred spirits, bloodied from love's warpath

Both relating on experiences buried deep in our past

I think I remember the moment when we sealed the deal

When we both yelled "Fuck it, can I just be real?"

Liberating, not giving a fuck about what was

A friendship is what we seeked, so it wasn't tough

That's when I realized that's what love is supposed to be

You're supposed to sit back and let your thoughts roam free

Trusting that person not to judge your demons

Thinking about that person all day for no reason

Not in love, but in love with the process of discovering love

And when I find it you'll be the one I think of

Because of our bond there has been a lot lessons gained

But most importantly we taught each other how to love again.

Terry Gingles

F.R.I.E.N.D.

Forever by your side, forever you and I,

Relating to each other's needs, hearing each other's cries.

Inside, my eternal flame burns for your happiness day by day,

Endless amounts of love, every minute I send your way.

Never out of sync, our convictions perfectly blend,

Delightful indeed is the soul, who inspired these words I pen

From The Start

I sit in my own form of hell

The only thing that comforts is the distant reminder of your smell.

Faint, vague and I can hardly tell

If this scent is pleasant or if is it stale.

I think I like it, 'cause it reminds me of fun times

But when I get real with myself it reminds me of what isn't mine.

So close to home, so close to completion

So close to love, circumstances it's intermission

That view… from the mountain top, I sat and starred.

Then the rain came, reminding how life wasn't fair.

It's hard to walk away, ignore the odds that play

Stevie's "Overjoyed", in unison with the waves that swayed

Low tide, pulling away all of my heat's feelings

My soul holding on, swept away as he struggles screaming

"I don't know", my answer when asked to love again

I didn't think I could before you, well, that was my plan

But obviously I can, proof, my broken heart

Just bad judgment on my end to get mixed up with you from the very start.

How dumb…

Hate

Why do you hate me? No seriously, I want to know why?

You're not really hiding how you feel, no matter how hard you try.

This isn't anything new, actually it's been going on for centuries.

My ancestors hundreds of years ago experienced the same thing you're doing to me.

And I just want to know why?

So I sat and thought then came to a conclusion.

And don't think I'm bragging or finding this amusing.

But you're scared of me, you're scared of what might be.

You're scared of what I do that comes pretty easy and naturally.

You're scared of my strength, you're scared of my resolve.

You're scared of my DNA that continues to evolve.

You're scared because it's you, who's truly the minority.

You put out destructive images in hopes to destroy me.

Turn the world against us, make other cultures hate their dark skin

Whitewash the population, you plotted while you grined.

Your genes are recessive, and there's proof when you mate

With anyone who's not you, your babies lose your traits

That has to be terrifying and I can't even blame you

I'm not saying any fables, it's just the honest truth.

I Got You

There's no better feeling than carving a smile into a wall of stone.

The only feeling that's better is convincing that wall that they're no longer alone.

I'll be your rock, lean on me whenever.

See I'm made of stone too, that's why to the mask you wear I'm clever.

That feeling of loneliness, yeah I've been there,

And I'd being lying if I said I didn't recognize that blank stare.

But I promised myself I'd change, open up my heart to the possibilities,

Embrace the unknown and rip up my old policies.

Take a risk and embrace these new rules,

And the first risk I want to take is one with you.

Give you all of me that I have to offer,

While I'm fixing my tie and adjusting my collar.

Clearing my throat asking "would you want to take this ride with me?"

"Close your eyes and let me guide you where you want to be."

"I got you..."

Backseat of My Uber

In the back seat of my Uber I see things I've never seen,

Like how the moonlight hits the clouds to cause a scene.

How the streetlights and stoplights shine so bright,

And how the air in this LA night hits so right.

But it's in the backseat sometimes that my mind can flow,

Where I lay my head back, not in control.

I live, I take a deep breath and breathe,

And not worry about this stress that bursting at seams.

Constricted, it seems that I can't seem to grow.

When I'm always driving around, living life on hope.

Scared Two

never knew what light was until you looked into my eyes.

Happiness now here, my fears demised.

I'm trying to be honest and real right now.

This smile I wear could never reverse to a frown.

I've been hurt before and those situations are tough.

You got me looking heartbreak in his eyes and calling his bluff.

Just the thought of your face inspires me daily,

Repairing my thoughts that have been stomped on gravely.

I wonder what do you think and how do you feel?

As I edge in close for a kiss to steal.

Does your heartbeat flutter? Does your face get warm?

Does that confidence you wear tend to lose its form?

At the thought of letting go and exploring this place

Or do you want to walk away and not leave a trace?

Deep down we want something real, that vision is shared,

But you can't reach for stars with hands that are scared.

So take me by the hand, see, they too tremble.

We'll cross this minefield, we'll be quick and nimble.

To fight for what we want we'll push and shove,

To have in our possession, this thing called love.

The Mirage

Mixed up, not knowing which way to go.

Mixed up, like the tequila in my blood flow.

Pumping me with memories, of what could be.

Pissing out the hate that those memories left me.

Some would say they're dreams, visions more than likely.

I say they're nightmares that only my brain can see.

Obviously I can't trust where my hearts wants to go.

Have me wandering in the desert searching for water that flows.

But it's not there, an illusion all in my mind.

A mirage of fakeness that I'll never find.

But for that split second when I see it, when it feels so real,

I have to go for it, reach for it, to see how it feels.

The hope of what's not there is better than what's here.

Because this reality of no love is what I truly fear.

Salty Trail

The tears have dried up and nothing left but a salty trail.

The anchor has been pulled up, as our dreams take sail.

That bitter taste in the air is caused by the death of many dreams.

They all retreat to this familiar place we call the sea.

In case you ever wondered how salt water came to be,

We tend to scream carpe diem yet the day is never seized.

The smile on a face is often misread,

It's usually the result of a love that's fled.

Ironically through a smile is how we bond.

How else can we safely make it thought this con?

Our pearly whites protect us from future pain,

And the cleansing of the rain keeps us sane.

But it never rains in the City of Angels,

And we can't help but be overtaken from the taste of salt from every angle.

People sinning, with blurred visions, no one's listening,

To the sounds of the hearts that have a beat skipping.

Terry Gingles

My First Time in the World

My first time in the world...

I remember the day,

I don't remember my age,

But I remember the stage.

I was a kid, and couldn't have been more than 4 or 5.

I sat by the door and plotted my stride.

For some reason I remember being in just my undies,

It was right before bath time after I filled my tummy.

The sun was setting and the sky was blue.

Pressed my face to the glass trying to figure what to do.

"Run!" I said, what was there to lose!?

I didn't have on any clothes nor wore any shoes.

I grabbed the door handle and began to push,

Leaned in with all my might, my face was smooshed!

Finally the door opened and it made a pop!

I ran outside but then I stopped.

"Oh my God, I'm out here all by myself...

These trees are so big" as the cool grass my feet felt.

I didn't even run, I just stood in awe ,

Everything was so quiet, I couldn't hear at all.

It all was so bright, vibrant and real,

It was my first view of the world, I had cracked the seal.

Just as I began to move my feet and started to glide

My mom yelled from the house "Boy, get back inside!"

Love Bliss

The stars in your eyes shine on me

Making my life so complete

Dark were my days,

Childish were my ways

Blinded by your eclipse

Mesmerized by your lips

I'm totally new to this

I now know what true love is

Love is not being able to sleep

When laying next to you

Cause I don't want to miss one moment

Every single second is brand new

Love is the comfort your scent brings

The song my heart sings

Knowing this isn't a fling

Encouraging me to stretch my wings

Flying next to you

Hand in hand

We're each others biggest fans

You being my lady, me being your man

Growing together, taking on the world

Moving mountains with thoughts

As together our minds twirled

No words can express how real this is

I've written many drafts and yet

Can't come up with ways to describe this bliss

Terry Gingles

Losing You

It kills me that I can't tell the world about you

It's a shame I can't brag on the things you do

It's not hard to tell I'm in a better place

It shines bright no matter how I hide my face

If I could I'd climb the highest mountain and yell you're the source

Let the world know you're the hottest flame in my torch

But soon my flame burns out

When these burning words in my heart I can't shout

At first, by all these secrets my brain was amused

But then my heart took over and called you his muse

Inspiring me with love, creation and patience

Wisdom and leadership in me, you create it

All the glory I want to give to you

And what comes from these traits I want to share with you

The skies' brightest shining star is how you make me feel

And if a heartbreak is what this cost, I'll foot the bill

Because at this moment right here and now, my lips are no longer sealed

And the benefits from this love I believe we should field

We only live once is the phrase that comes to mind

when I say fuck the rules, I want to make you mine

A million friendships isn't worth the one love I'd lose

and that's a chance I can't take if that means losing you

Terry Gingles

Easy To Fall For You

It's so easy to fall in love with you,

A number of casualties have fallen and I'll be one of the few.

I get lost in your eyes, your soft skin reels me in,

I think about you all the time, in a flutter my heart spins.

I sit and smile when I think about the way you sway,

The memory of your scent keeps me in a daze.

The echoes of your giggle bounce against the walls in my head,

And the sparkle from your smile is what keeps my soul fed.

Misunderstood, is what I think you are,

But I want to figure you out though this task is hard.

I often wonder what you think when it comes to me?

Am I just a toy you play with once a week?

I don't know the answer and quite frankly don't care,

Is what I tell myself as deeply in your eyes I stare.

Cause when I'm with you nothing in this world matters,

You can tell I'm happy by my bruised cheeks from laughter.

This truly was an endless summer, my nights spent with you,

Gave me a reboot on life as off the edge I flew.

I've become a better man through your encouraging words and support.

When I began to write this, I had plans on keeping it short.

But I can't, just like I can't imagine my life without you.

That strength from your hugs comforts like morning dew.

Oh I just want to love you, and love you the right way!

I close my eyes and remember how on my chest you laid,

And how good that felt, I never wanted it to end.

I stayed up and watched you sleep, you were my girl in pretend,

But sadly you and I will probably never be...

It has nothing to do with what you offer and it doesn't fall on me.

Circumstances, rules, there are some lines we should never cross.

But I would if I could be forever in your love, lost.

Terry Gingles

I Can Hardly Wait

I can't control the feelings I have inside

Whenever we're close my heart just glides

My heart beat races, for love it chases

Off the potential of happiness that it's tasted

Just the thought of you warms me up

And the scent of you has me stuck

In the place I wish I always was

Second to only the heavens above

I get so lost when I look in your eyes

I shake cause the real me can no longer hide

Complete is the feel, believe its real

I could no longer conceal, the way I feel

Calm I slept with my palm on your waist

When these dreams come true, I can hardly wait

Forever Mine

That moment I closed my eyes and kissed you

I knew I was traveling down a road of sin.

The softness of your breath, the taste of your mouth,

Had my heart race, as my lust for you caressed your skin.

The whiff of your natural scent drove me crazy.

Making me connect with my animal instincts,

Forcing my decision making to become hazy.

We shouldn't have done that thing we did.

But when that spark is lit,

It's hard not to follow the road of that illuminated grid. We're going to hell and I don't mind (smirk).

At least down there we'll be together,

And you will forever be mine.

Terry Gingles

Even Though It's Right

Can we slow down and seize the moment,

In this happy place that isn't cracked or broken

The special ones aren't always promised

Here is the place where we can finally be honest

Every day feels like something new

Relying on each other is all we knew

Incomplete I feel when you're not around

Not one moment with you am I ever down

Ever felt like you have met the one

Don't know the reason but you know you've won

Only catch to this, it could never be

Even though it's right and so plain to see

Due Time

When trapped in a corner, them dogs, they will bite

Scraps on the floor, believe me they'll fight

Whether it's friend or foe maybe bitch or hoe

You'll be stooped and perplexed not knowing where to go

Fear is stronger than love, that's what Pac told me

Tatted it on my arm, insurance, for future enemies

Then hate reared its ugly face and took loves place

Never thought it would come disguised in a smiling friends face

I see the pain in your heart, the fear in your eyes

When you look in the mirror, you see me personified

And that scares you, cause there can only be one

You can't use tungsten lights to replace the sun

But it is what it is, I knew it back then

I guess I felt sorry for you when I took you in as friend

We can draw the lines, like the part in a spine

Or we can patch it up now praying it will be fine

It doesn't matter to me, I'ma still be me

That's what got me where I am, it's what set me free

But who are you? Do you really know?

Terry Gingles

Do you love who you are? I'll assume that's a no.

And that really sucks, because who you are is cool

I just wish you saw, and believed it was true

But until then, I gots to go out to get mine

And we'll figure this out within due time

Started Loving You

Sitting here thinking

About the best ways to describe love

Staring at this blank page

Until it was you I thought of

Now I don't think you should come to mind

When describing this feeling

I've never even kissed your lips

Yet the thought of you is healing

Being around you I grow

Reaching the potential of a man

I feel this deep calm inside of me

Alone, never again I'll stand

If you were mine,

Gat damn I'd be at ease

Nothing else in the world would matter

I'd take in your breeze

Your feeling is cool

Yet warm when I'm open

To give you all of me

Terry Gingles

My heart feels unbroken

Able to fully love again

A feeling I thought never to be true

A feeling that laid dormant

Until the day I started loving you

Paws and Strings

I'm there strictly for her entertainment

The feline paws me back and forth

And if I'm lucky I may get a lick

And every so often I get tangled in her claws

That's when she shows me extra attention

Not because she wants to

The feeling of me stuck in her claws is annoying to her

But the time she takes to untangle us is precious to me

Because at least it's time with her

She's paying me attention

One on one

Yeah I know

I deserve better

But the shit feels good tho

So go fuck ya self

Terry Gingles

In Your Lust

I was baptized

In your lust

The water filled my ears

My brain, I couldn't trust

Wet, I can bet

Not the first to fail this test

Now I'm here

The F's for fear

Now the only wetness I feel are tears

Ran through,

Abused and used

My heart is stripped

Like a nail, I'm no use

Spinning in circles, inside the wood

Thought I was moving but in place I stood

Dizzy I became

There is no shame

The wild animal you are

I could never have tamed

But your poison, damn, I mean lust

Had me trying to reach places that I couldn't touch

Terry Gingles

My Little Albino Friend

My little albino friend

Only comes out when

I'm feeling good

When all is well

He creeps in my world

And steals all my food

All my happiness,

all my joy

All my smiles

He kicks them over

Puts his feet up

Then stays for a while

Causing chaos is his specialty

No sun in his world

So he pulls light from me

Leaving me drained

Mad at everything

No explanation for my pain

His laughs sound like liquid

Pouring in my favorite glass

Away I now go

He holds my head,

Props me up

To make sure I get in the door

He only wants me to be successful so he can reunite with his friends

The ones of the people I hang out with, in their brains his friends live.

But that I can't give

For him, I can't give my time

So he reluctantly craws up my arm

Back in that dark place I call my mind

Terry Gingles

The Relationship

You're a dirty and filthy whore
Who only bathes during high tide with your tear-filled shores.
Hobos, homos, schizos with afros roam the street
Walking past people with masks, plastic and meek.
With their tattooed smiles and permanent frowns
Screams and weeping are your ambient sounds.
Your scent is weird, a mixture of flavors
Of piss and weed and street dogs that savor.
The broken stars on the boulevard, concrete that's cracked
Broken dreams from broken teens from which love they lacked
The City of Angels, depends on which angle
You look at her cause her wings are mangled.
But the sun shines daily, some call it her halo
You can close your eyes and with you she'll tango
Dance you off into an euphoric bliss
And then drop you off on route 66
Then you'll open your eyes, broke and blue
Realizing you were in love with a bitch who never loved you.

Los Angeles

You Only Get One

You only get one...

Others say that's not true

But tell that to your heart who remains black and blue

You only get one

Only one can make your heart race

Only one will make you speed up your pace

Only one in your dreams you will see

Only one makes you cry when they don't come to be

You only get one

You know it when you see it

But don't want to retrieve it

You only get one

Scared to admit it

Trying to force yourself to resist it

You only get one

Terry Gingles

You held them in your arms

Should have heard the alarms

You only get one

But arrogance won't think that's true

Fool you into thinking that you will get two, but

You only get one

When you have that one

Don't neglect that one

You may think its fun

But end up with none

You only get one

The Day The Mermaid Drowned

I close my eyes and see her swimming, across the ocean blue.

Her light brown eyes, and sandy colored hair accompanied her graceful mood.

She would glide through the sea, just like a breeze, as her tail parted the water

The salt exfoliated her smooth brown skin, causing other fish to falter.

The woman of their dreams, these men would see, while on their nautical journeys.

They'd come to shore with tales to tell, on how they all adored thee

But the love she got, from those who loved, could not stand the test.

As far as she knew, she was deformed, and always felt second best.

So when the sun would set, to the depths she'd go, down to the ocean floor.

To the bottomless pit, she had the key, to open the devils door.

Looking for answers, pressing the issue, to fill the void inside

Altering her mind, from things unkind, causing her soul to cry.

When she finally resurfaced and tried to swim, I saw the pain within.

I docked my boat and dove right in, forgetting that I could not swim

A struggle ensued, now she's confused, questioning my motives to help.

She fought me off, and began to weep, releasing a screeching yelp.

Terry Gingles

I release her hand and close my ears, deaf from the painful sound.

She was no longer seen, bubbles filled the sea, proof that the mermaid had drowned.

Stuff

Plastics, paper, rubber and metal,

All stuff we own to make us feel better.

It feels like the more we have the emptier we feel,

And I'm including myself amongst the ones not real.

More than half this shit I don't even use.

Yet I cling to these things like I've been abused.

Consumerism and capitalism are my masters.

Slaves to others' desires so we tend to spend faster.

Souls, oops, I mean currency exchanges each transaction.

Spending more than we have, hoping for traction.

But we slip, slip further down the hole,

No way to make it back because we can't afford the toll.

Stuck in a simulation, our fossils fueling the enterprise,

Can't sugar coat this shit no matter how hard we try.

Life and love are the only things that are real,

These two invisible L's are the only things we actually feel.

Terry Gingles

Right now I cry

Right now I cry

There's no rhyme or season to the shit

I couldn't begin to tell you why

Well perhaps there's a thing or two

That when I dwell on them

They turn me blue

Being alone, no love in sight

Knowing I'm not ready for that

With these inner demons I fight

My brains feels stuck when switching gears

Can't grasp the simple things in life

Beyond living in fear

Biggest Fear

My biggest fear is amounting to nothing.

I'm working and using my talents, trying to become something.

I've seen it many times before, people fail going for the unattainable

I'm not trying to be one of those dudes, I'm bringing something to the table

Though unstable and shaky, it may break me,

I refuse to quit even though the finish line I can't see

I'm slowly dying, with only an ounce of hope left.

My blood pumps slow, with a slight beat in my chest.

It may appear fun, it may appear slick,

But believe me, I'm a disappointment away from a slit wrist.

And I'm not just talking shit, this pain is so real

I often bite my tongue to see if I still feel.

Most of the time I don't, I live in a numb state,

This regimen I'm on, I need to update.

I'm at a crossroads and I can go either way

Become the best ever, or hang in a hallway

Self-inflicted wound, and I mean the permanent kind

The one that you make, there's no kind of rewind

Terry Gingles

"How can you talk like this?" is what you will ask.

"You seem to have it together and on the right path."

Ain't shit right, and that's the honest truth

I haven't loved myself since about 2002

Right now I'm feeling low, with nowhere to go

At this moment I can't cope, there's no hope

I'm done

Get Off On The Pain

I must get off on this pain

Because there's no way else I'd stay the same

Insane, drained and nothing to gain

From traveling down this dark road time and time again

Taking the test, knowing the answers

Inhaling the smoke, enjoying the cancer

The tumors, the welts, the bruises within

Knowing right from wrong and yet I sin

I'm pinned in a corner with no where to go

Well there's a place to go, but can't take that road

'Cause the road less traveled is the one I want

And the voice in my head knows but taunts

Me with a vision where I some how win

Knowing deep down inside it's a dead end

I Don't Know...

I don't know why I'm sad

I don't know why I cry

I don't know why I'm mad

I don't know why I sigh

I don't know why I see clouds when the sun shines

Look, I don't know

I don't know why I don't want to leave the house

I don't know why I can't to get off the couch

I don't know why I often pout

I don't know why I feel left out

I told you, I don't know

I don't know why I feel small

I don't know why I always fall

I don't know why I feel this is it

Hell, I don't know why I even wrote this shit

I don't know...

If I Can Make It Through the Night

If I can just make it through the night,

Come morning everything will be better.

If I can just make it through the night,

I would have survived this stormy weather.

My four walls are closing in.

My patience is wearing thin.

My light inside is growing dim.

"It will be better tomorrow," my thoughts within.

If I can just make it through the night,

Tomorrow will be a new day.

These dark thoughts will have no place to stay,

And the happy ones will be allowed to play.

My phone is silent, my inbox is empty,

Terry Gingles

Not a soul in sight out there to help me.

I'm trying to make it through the night.

To make matters worse I fell asleep around eight,

Work up at midnight, now I'm up, that's great.

I'm going to be up all night.

Throwing back vodka, neat to be exact.

Music plays in the background to keep my soul intact.

As I make it through the night.

No money to my name, while trying to remain sane.

Using this last match to re-spark my flame.

To make it through the night.

Me all alone, with evil thoughts that roam.

I wish they were homeless or at least didn't use my brain as their home,

Because they'll be up all night.

Daydreams of bliss.

Perhaps a blueprint for how to treat this.

During this never ending night

I close my eyes to think,

_____

The birds are chirping and now it's dawn.

I passed out asleep with all the lights on.

I guess I made it through the night.

I reread my words as I rock and sway.

Disappointed now, because I still feel the same way.

Can I make it through the day?

Small Steps

I could have gone to sleep

But I didn't want to punk out

I wanted to look her dead in the face

Knowing I could have got up and forced a date

But I didn't

I sat here by myself

Read a couple chapters from some new books I got

I checked the clock a few times when I got antsy

But I closed my computer and kept reading

2 A.M. hit and I was in the clear

it was my first victory at the top of the year.

Feels Normal

My feelings are numb

Or that's what I think, they could be just dormant.

Waiting around for the perfect time to peek their head out.

I fool myself to think it's progress, this no feeling thing.

I try to think about the things that make me sad and nothing comes to mind,

And I wish it would just so I could get past it.

But nothing.

Damn do I feel anything?

Maybe that's why I do consume so much, so I can feel.

Feel my pulse, feel my brain working, feel connected.

There's nothing worse that not being able to feel.

I'd rather have a heartbreak or an anxiety attack, something!

But this no feeling shit is for the birds.

I blame my sober mind,

And it's because of this sober mind I haven't written in days.

But today I freed him and wrote.

It feels good, it feels... normal.

Better Man

I drove around Burbank just to get out of the house

I had errands to run and of course I could have run those in the morning

But I convinced myself right now was the time to leave.

Deposited a 10 dollar check and stopped by Ralphs.

"oh not now, I don't have the time"

what I said when I spotted a homeless guy in front of the store

I make it inside with a direct line towards self-destruction.

Paced up and down the aisle confirming I wanted to make this purchase.

I did,

Then proceeded to pay.

On my way out and I saw something,

The nerdiest nerd taking time to talk to that same homeless guy.

At first it made sense, two lonely souls connecting.

I hop in my car and turn the ignition,

Sit for a second and start thinking.

As I watch them both share a laugh,

The only lonely person in this parking lot is me.

That nerd and that homeless guy

In that moment, that day

Were also better men than me.

Respect

HerStory

She moved to LA with dreams of hitting it big

18 years ago, and still ain't found a gig.

I know you've heard this story before but that version was bland,

I'm telling you this account I've seen first hand.

Her open eyes were bright, gracefully she'd glide,

chasing the dreams she held from deep inside.

Not knowing that it wasn't meant to be,

But you can't tell a blind person things they can see.

Because their other senses are heightened, enlightened and potent,

and don't have time for guidance from those who seem broken.

So down this road she'd pursue,

having turned her back on everything she knew.

She partied with the elite, her lips were always puckered,

kissing a billion dollars' worth of lips, labeled star fucker.

But left with nothing tangible to show,

no dough, feeling low with their leftover blow.

Meaningless kisses on the forehead, no love to show,

the soundtrack to her life were her flushed dreams down the commode.

As she lay balled up in a blanket with time to think,

while another avenue washed up and rinsed off in her sink.

If she could blink and was allowed three wishes she'd laugh,

She'd nail it all at once, all she needed was a draft.

She would say out loud and proud "just to make it",

and pray that her past to all who witnessed was forsaken.

But those roots run deep, their foundation was self-hate,

instead of using her mind, she used her body to cast bait.

Hoping with the odds on her side they would eventually subside,

and her fears would hide and her dreams would abide.

But so far those visions weren't allowed a chance,

and now she hears the music at her last dance.

With a dude who gets off on her pain and feuds,

I knew it from the jump that it was bad news.

Because he dangled everything that she thought she needed,

and with her clock ticking it was now time to get seeded.

So she proceeded with an open mind and of course open legs,

not knowing this decision she would forever dread.

Because no fucks were given, he proceeded to cast demons

on my friend's brain, which was open like the season.

She believed him, when he said it was love,

Terry Gingles

as he had her on her on knees with his gun shoved,

to the side of her head, her integrity shed,

forcing her to watch videos showing him getting head

from other girls in his spell, her eyelids did swell,

images now forever dwell in her living hell.

When she escaped from the place she sighed and cried,

He didn't know she took his gun and hid it inside

that very same bag that he bought and flaunted,

giving her false dreams of what he thought she wanted.

Standing in the mirror, she hated who she saw,

mumbling to herself this was the very last straw.

She pulled out the gun, she held it with anger,

thinking she owed herself this one last favor.

As she squeezed the trigger she released the stress,

Tired of losing in her dreams, at last a success.

A tree fell feel that day, yet nobody knows,

no sounds were made, resting in its final pose

I propose when you see a person look past their grin,

Because we all have a story that's killing us within.

Reflection

I stare in the mirror and look at my face

Study my features as my fingers begin to trace

Full lips noted, broad nose, check

The brown skin that I'm in I began to stretch

Search these nooks and crannies, I even looked behind my ear

To see what's buried deep that's causing you to fear.

It must be something, because your anger is dialed in.

Got me feeling a type of way 'cause my patience has worn thin

Now never did I believe where we lived was post racial

But I had a glimmer of hope that it was at least stable

But that tiny crack in the windshield has finally spread

Killing after killing, it's all come to a head.

I can't walk without stares, can't drive without looks.

I can't shop with no cares, they worry I'm a crook.

But that's what they tell you, got to be more to this story

It's like they got some kind of results from a laboratory.

Because the fears escalated, oops, I mean violence.

Something has been learned for you not to remain silent

Terry Gingles

I wonder what it was that made you insecure

Perhaps it was my strength or maybe my allure.

How I keep standing and proud at that.

No matter how hard you try I'm still proud to be Black.

Yes I'm gifted, smart and full of resolve

And yes I'm creative with these problems I continue to solve.

And no matter how many times I'm down, or the times that I'm struck

I will always discover the strength to stand back up.

Question the Power

Up in the brisk cold sky those cold faces stare,

Palms in the air while casting out prayers.

Looking for answers, a sign of some sort,

Avoiding eye contact from those there to thwart.

Because if that connection is made, miscued as being cold,

An unleashing of anger, pent-up ,will unfold.

Because truth be told, marching may not be the solution.

While some will say "Well, neither is looting."

And you know what? You're right, there's no need for these things.

That is, if you cared more about all human beings.

And you have to admit that does come out odd,

Especially from those who claim they love God.

So I have a right to bare stares, arms and fist,

And unravel these facts you tie up and twist.

Because the truth of the matter that's clear in my head,

I may as well do something because I can still end up dead.

Laid out on the concrete for the whole world to see,

What happens when you rightfully confront the powers that be.

Terry Gingles

My Hands Are Up

My hands are up, that means don't shoot.

My hands are up, which means I didn't loot.

My palms face the sky, my expression screams why?

My shirt is wet, soaking up tears from those who cry.

Open season, the season is open on black males.

The thought of living free has now become stale.

We have no clue what it means to live and be free,

To be able to walk worry-free and embrace whom we be.

Because propaganda brainwashed you about who I am!

News stories and television lied to you about my stance!

The confidence scares you, and the frame intimidates,

The stride makes you shake and the strength you hate.

But it's not our problem, clearly it's all yours.

The chickens are home to roost, the ones you ignored.

Maybe it's a revolution or just a fight for equality,

Tired of being stepped on and pushed into poverty.

Broken schools, broken homes and broken dreams

Reading back on our history to discover what it means,

To be black, to be African, to find my rightful place.

To discover what you know about me that makes you want to hate.

My hands are up...

Terry Gingles

I Can't Breathe

"I can't breathe!"

It's like we're the ones who forgot survival

and now it's our turn being stuck while our hands hold these Bibles

"I can't breathe..."

The last words spoken by our brother,

Camera's rolling while he's choking, the world stares at the smother.

"I can't breathe?"

Harassed for a lucy or a single,

police got him hemmed up as their shirts get wrinkled

"I... can't breathe"

And you think this still a game,

spending money on these Jordans and these weaves with no shame

"...can't breathe

Others wonder what's the fuss

while their kin get one up, with no fucks about us

"...breathe"

Is all we really want to do,

live life how we do, stick and move how we chose

"..."

I'm dead

Trolling For Love

I almost want to get back with you so I can feel again

Something is better than nothing so bring on your pain

Bring on your headaches, your bitching and lack of maturity

Deep down, I know it, feeds my insecurities

You're a habit I just can't seem to quit

And your cocky grin, proof, you're sure of it

I lie to myself and say I'm in control

But my soul knows, I'm just feeding a troll

For a while I was strong out on my own

But then Adele came on, just singing our song

Had me thinking about times from our past

And maybe this time it could truly last

I pick up the phone and stare at your name

Knowing if I call, I'm the only one to blame

So I put it down and take a sip of this rosé

Satisfied that this troll won't eat off me today

Toy Box

Alone in the toy box I sit

Amongst the other toys forgotten and quit

Collecting dust, loose joints and tangled

Some of us have been abused, used and mangled

Forgotten was the joy we brang

Our praises, they no longer sang

Our purpose was served, now we're old

In darkness we lay, our stories untold

There's only so much you can take being shunned and forgotten

Can't ignore the stench from your soul that's withered and rotten

I wish I could ignite this bomb accessory I came with, nestled between these blocks

Put to rest myself and everyone else inside this box

At least then we could melt away and become free

Perhaps take form and shape into who we were meant to be

Just when I'm at my peak fantasizing about the end

The door opens and we receive love from all their friends

Loved and played with like never before

I was the toy they never got that they always wished for

A new lease on life, purpose given again

I feel alive once more and I'm not feeling insane

It took their love for me to realize I wasn't the problem

I let someone else opinion dictate why I'd fallen

I was just being me, as I laid there and was discovered

I had a lot of love left to give is what they uncovered

A lifetime of joy in me is what they saw

I'm sure glad I didn't ignite that ole bomb of mine that could have ended it all

Terry Gingles

Dormant

I thought I quit you

I thought my love for you was through

I felt like I moved on

I felt as though I had grown

But damn when I hear that song

All that thinking I was doing is proven wrong

Dormant were my feelings for you

Dormant is where lay the truth

Dormant.

Tucked away were my feelings

Tucked away was the meaning,

The meaning of life you gave me

The keys to life that set me free

Introduced me to abstract ways of thinking

And I only stand here now cause you're the reason

Dormant my feelings were

Dormant I could have swore

That my love for you had come to an end

Now I stand before you making amends

I'm Tired

I'm tired

I'm tired of you

I'm tired of how you eat

I'm tired of how you sleep

I'm tired of the shit you spew

I'm tired of your hair

I'm tired of your stares

I'm tired of pretending to care

I am motherfucking tired

I'm tired of the force

The force it takes to hold this together

I'm tired of worrying that your love is fair weather

The part of you that has grown into me I want to sever

Hopeful I was

Hopeful that you were the one

Hopeful you were the one I dreamed of

Hopeful that it was the right choice because it made sense

But cents times 10,000 is what it's cost me

And I mean in years not just currency

I don't think I pretended to be anything I wasn't

But I cannot resist this urge to vomit

Or purge I should say, purge this cancer out of me

Down the toilet to eternity

But I just can't

I can't quit you

I can't leave you

Unfortunately because I love you

Fuck you

Eternal Flame

My eternal flame forever beats to the rhythm of your heart

Though miles, time and life has kept us apart

No way ever will I be allowed to hold you in my arms again

For vowels you have shared with your destined man

Not mad, no hate or animosity do I have

Towards you, your life or your better half

I just hold on to the thoughts and memories in my mind

Of when life was easy and I believed you were mine

The whole world I held, oh man did I have it all

I was able to kiss you good night from winter to fall

But the weather changes and the leaves lose life

As they fall high from the sky and out of plain sight

My love, my feelings my heart I describe

My pain oozes from my chest like honey from a hive

Walk towards me fast and stung you will be

Because the workers in my hive still protect the queen bee

But little do they know that she is dead

And the one they protect is just a myth in their head

She used to live here, and spread her wings she did

Flying around my heart, though the keys I hid

She never could relax, I made it unsafe for her to land

Entertaining other bees, my false measures of a man

And now here I stand, still alone, she sees

Counting her blessings the day she up and left me

Her honey, oh her honey was as sweet as can be

Never again will I enjoy the buzz from that bee

Terry Gingles

I Don't Have The Energy To Cry

I don't have the energy to cry,

Believe me, I tried and tried and tried.

But they're stuck, held up by sense,

Though my heart is still on the fence.

You were my boo,

The one I gave my heart to,

But I'm through.

I'm afraid this love can't continue.

Hurts, cause I felt you were the one.

Now I'm the one screaming that we're done.

Empty space, voided heart,

Should have known this was doomed from the start.

It's been weeks now and yet these tears I can't release.

These tears of hurt have become perspiration of peace.

Cool as a fan, just waiting on His plan,

Where I find my lady that completes me as a man.

No pressure, these shoes that are left vacant,

They're not broken in yet since the last one faked it.

Still smell new, look new, and wear new,

But the right size fits only a few.

This challenge I put out to you I'm glad you accept,

Because I was about to throw away all the answers to my test.

And you aced it, there was no need for a curve.

And your prize is all of me, and that's my word.

Funny how life works when you think about it.

Gotta drop all your baggage so you're free to lift.

Sometimes I wish this would have happened sooner,

But I needed time to reflect and reject this loser.

But it is what it is because you're here now,

Not worried about the past, too busy living in the now.

Terry Gingles

When The Smoke Clears

When the smoke clears

And those dried up tears

Cease to exist

Along with my fears

There you stood

Under my nose

This whole time

Comforting woes

Two and two never merged

The bat was blind

My anxiety purged

I took the time

To open my eyes

To see you standing

By my side

86

I'd be a fool

Not to think

What could be

If we linked

I know we're friends

That's who we are

But I'll admit

My tissue scars

At the thought

At not giving it a try

Butterflies fly

And I don't know why

I guess because

With you I'm home

I can be myself

And no longer roam

Terry Gingles

We may not be

Each other's perfect fit

But something's there

Though just a bit

And that small bit

Fits like a glove

And it's got me thinking

Could it be love?

Mona's Smile

Salt water in the air as it blows your hair

Through the messiness I found your face and stare

My own Mona Lisa and I caused the grin

And I did it all out of love with a hint of sin

A natural bond, it was real easy to stick

I knew that was the case before I kissed your lips

California Deserts

In the deep California deserts the stars above shine bright,

But when in the city where angels dwell I seem to always search for a light.

These dark blue days seem to always overwhelm my thoughts,

The scar tissue around my heart proves how hard I fought.

Then you stepped in my life, a horizon to better days,

Clearing out those cloudy thoughts that often left me dazed.

Making me a better person, anticipating what tomorrow brings.

Waking up in the morning, accompanying the blue bird that sings.

Happiness and joy, a deep appreciation for life.

Things I couldn't comprehend until you came and shined your light

Light or Dark

I told her "we attract what we are.

So I guess we better figure out if it's the light or dark side of our souls that's driving this connection,

Before it's too late".

Bathing

You don't want to be the one, the one who forces me to create,

Because most of my stimulation is born from hate.

So when you see me at ease and my attitude is chill,

It's because I'm bathing in your love that's feeling so real.

Breaking The Seal

The mere thought of you forces me to want to create my greatest creation

The scent of you puts my mind at work with no hesitation

You helped turn my blacks, blues and browns

Into dancing yellows and purples inside of my crown

Good isn't a good enough word to use

I feel so alive when I'm with you

The true definition of a muse

Pure as the clo

uds and angel tears fused

Rain on me, bathe me

You baptize me effortlessly

Born again in the name of love

Terry Gingles

After being killed before by a poisoned one

Built me up though you didn't even know it

Never touched you, only caressed your spirit.

And that was enough... for now... I think

I threw my hands up as I began to sink

Down the rabbit hole, the further I go

My courage grows and so does my hope

That this feeling I have is real

Because I'm beyond ready to break the seal

Flaws and all

That crooked smile and sleepy eyes

Traits I usually wouldn't fall for but feelings never lie

It's that confidence of yours

That I couldn't ignore

I could learn to adore

And would never be bored

Cause I like you

I was intimidated by the gap

In age, so I adapt

Your intrigue never lacks

Impossible to hold back

It's really true

To me, you're so cool

That walk of yours

The way you sway

The way you laugh

Terry Gingles

I don't want to stray

I'm locked in on you

The way you sound

When close and near

Sticks in my brain

You're always near

Yeah, I dig you

The talks we have

that last all night

I can't deny

This feeling is right

I hope it's the same for you

The Reason Why

Those oils and incense fill up the room

She smells like the earth

And that's what made me take notice

Soil and fresh rain

Healthy dirt where I could plant my pain

Her bushy hair catches all my bull shit

As I fall into place and rest my face on her belly

No time to dwell on insecurities that tend to bully

She makes me feel like a king

And what that makes me do

Is go out in the world and want to provide

Keep a smile on her face

Lace her with happiness

As I gaze at her like a queen

My rib

My oak tree

Providing me oxygen

Terry Gingles

So I can survive

My Nefertiti

I fix her headpiece

To make sure the world can see the perfection I see

My spinach

She pops eyes

So when you see me shinning

She's my reason why

Swipe Right

I keep knocking at your door and there's no answer

This ole anxiety of mine is eating away like cancer

Yes I did mess up, you don't think I remembered

I was drunk one night so I browsed around Tinder

But that doesn't mean I didn't believe in us

That doesn't mean that I betrayed our trust

It's just that I was feeling lonely one night

And was searching for a feeling that felt right

Never could I ever replace you with one swipe right

And just know I'm not losing you without a fight

That sunshine in your eyes eclipsed my heart

The thought of losing you tears me apart

I start to think of the days that were good

When our short hand was synch and perfectly understood

Laughs and giggles that were shared

When you caught me lost in you with my stare

Seeing this future of mine with you

Visualizing my future works of which you'd muse

This is just a rough patch that hopefully we get through

I just hope that on the other side you'll see my love for you was true

Terry Gingles

Finished The Race

I see it in your eyes,

So much talent with no ambition

And I get it, you don't have time for that.

Never mind the time we spent together

Laughing, smoking, fucking and laughing

At the end of the day it's the drive you see

And for the moment I probably didn't have much.

But there's a reason for that.

And that reason was that moment I met you it felt good

It felt amazing.

I hadn't felt that in a minute and I thought I had every right to just lay in that for a while.

You know, take it in

Smell it, breathe it, love it, dream

It's something I had been chasing for years

And it appeared this might be it.

Ahhhh, I just forgot how you dames work.

You like drive, love ambition.

And which you should, that's in your DNA.

So when you looked at me you saw my eyes were full of love, ready to give

But they appeared to lack that drive

Just know I was making room for you

Because I know putting all my efforts into making money isn't the top goal

And for me to be who I need to be in my corner I need the right girl.

It was only a pit stop

I needed an oil change to finish the race

But you bailed out early, without a trace

I dig it...

I had no problems letting go

I'm afraid my heart doesn't work at full speed anymore

The Break up: Closure

I can't put my finger on it

But whatever it was

On that day

In that moment

We knew

It was over...

The Long Goodbye

Our eyes connected through a reflection

The mirror still had a thin layer of condensation from your shower

Yet clearly we still saw each other

No words were spoken

But everything was said

In our gaze

For a minute

In silence

We stood

Weighing the good and the bad

The latter won

You knew it and so did I

Damn four months, we had a pretty good run

You agreed

I saw it in that slight twinkle in your eye

Yet we arrived at the same conclusion

You're not the one for me

Nor am I the one for you

So farewell my dear

Terry Gingles

Perhaps, maybe... next lifetime

we'll meet as butterflies

Don't worry Mama

I'm fine

I'll let myself out

The Dame on Dickens

The Fall of 2014 will always remain close to my heart

It was during that time, from you, I never wanted to part

Laughs and catch phrases we shared... "listen"

It was during this time I fell for a "Dame on Dickens"

Small in stature but her presence was huge

Quickly at the heart I felt we were fused

Happiness was in my eyes when I looked at you

The happiness you gave had me searching for truth

Sad how a red flag can end a good thing

But sometimes you have to listen when the fat lady sings

Maybe we could have worked if we continued to believe

If we removed our fears we could have achieved

For whatever the reasons we discontinued our growth

I understand the decision but I want you to know

All those imperfections in yourself that you see

Didn't matter at all because you were always perfect to me

Terry Gingles

For What

Sitting here thinking

About the feeling

I don't have no more

Sitting here wishing

It was you

I could love some more

Some things aren't meant to be

But that thing was never supposed to be you and me

We had it all covered and planned

I got off on the fact that you loved me and called me your man

You were my rib

I now don't know what gives

Why it couldn't work, why it didn't last

I thought we gave everything we had

Maybe it wasn't enough

Maybe we didn't have true love

Maybe were we scared

Scared to give all of us

I do know, I've never given that much

Of myself that I fell out of touch

With reality, losing connection as this world spins

You were in my atmosphere, your solar winds

Blew me away, your beauty one of a kind

More than the physical, mostly your mind

Is what had me, your mate was in check

Forced me to rethink the goals I had set

Because they were now a bundle, dreams for two

I wanted to create the perfect life for me and you

Give you room to grow and reach your full potential

All outlined with my heart's stencil

But for whatever reason it ended

Those love votes we cast were rescinded

Overruled, voted down, Lord knows why

Overthinking this situation and potentially destroying our lives

For what?

That Itch

I was told that love is itch that's in the palm of hand.

You know, the one that's there but impossible to scratch!

Oh you don't think that's love?

Really?

Well perhaps I should go get this checked out.

#mindfuck

When you're hurt and the pit of your soul is empty,

You'd be surprised at what you'll use to satisfy that vacant feeling.

You'll violate rules,

Substances you'll abuse,

Reality and fantasies you'll fuse,

Instant gratification you'll choose.

It takes some time,

Where you can take a step back and take it all in.

And what really hurts,

What reopens the wound,

Is that safe haven you thought you found,

What you put your faith and love in,

Is nothing but a mirage.

#mindfuck

(She sweetly whispers in my ear "you're welcome")

Terry Gingles

Still here

I love being me

I love everything about it

I love my broad wide nose

I love my earth tone skin

I love my kinky hair grows up

Up towards the light

Tickling the toes of the gods

I love how I come from a line of strong people

It gives me strength to keep pushing forward

To be the best I can be

I love how love is in my DNA

And no matter how hard they try

They can't beat, cover or murder that out of me

There's a lot to be said of a people who have gone through what we have

And how through all the pain, we're still here

Sun Kissed

The sun rose

Then smiled on me

I awoke

And realized it was your smile that shined on thee

Your vitamin D soaked into my pores

That melanin of mine

Made it easy to store

A place of warmth

That high yellow glow

Fills me to the brim

I can't seem to say no

Terry Gingles

Those Ole Lonely Souls

Those ole lonely souls

You can't hide

No matter how hard you try to blend in

I see you

For I too struggle

I wear a mask

I laugh

I smile

I help others

I create works that put others at ease

But once I'm home

It's back to my tornado of destruction

There's no need for me to explain

We both know

You think you're concealed

But it's all in the eyes

Those never lie

My head nod to you isn't to say what's up

It's to say you're not alone

We're together on this lonely path called life

Acknowledgements

This is going to be a long list. I have so many people to thank and show appreciation to so bare with me.

I'd like to first thank God. We're all born with talents and I thank you daily for giving me the vision to discover mine. I also want thank you for blessing me with the best family and friends on earth!

My Parents, Terry Sr. and Mildred Gingles. I love playing around with words but become speechless once attempting to express how much your love means to me. Without you I am nothing. I count my blessings everyday and I am thankful being your son. Your infinite love, encouragement, patience and support gets me through the day, heck it gets me through my life. I love you both dearly!

My sister, Kimborah Ann Croom. I love the heck out of you! I am so proud of the woman, wife and mother you have become! You have always been amazing to me. Even though I'm your big brother, I look up to you! You have always carried yourself with intelligence and grace. I love you!

My Brother-in-Law, Randall Croom. It never seems to fail whenever we're around each other we always seem to have a four-hour conversation, from which I always take something positive away from and apply it in my life. I'm proud of everything you have accomplished! This book wouldn't exist if it weren't for you. From the bottom of my heart, thank you!

My nephew, Knox Power Croom. I love you Man! You can and will become whatever it is in the world you want to be! You are smart. You are talented. You are loved!

The Gingles, Moore and Jackson Family. We roll deep and there are too many of us to name but I love you all. You all inspire me to work hard and be the best I can be. There is no other way our family knows how to operate but being amazing. Like granddad said "y'all better stick". That goes for everyone I share the same DNA with. I love you all! Michael Futch thank you for being the closest thing to a brother I've had. I'm proud of everything you've become. Keep defying the odds Man.

All my friends from Indianapolis, Indiana. Thank you guys for your continued love and support. I wouldn't be who I am if it weren't for the good morals and values I learned growing up in the Hoosier state. Tamika Knox, thank you for being a true friend and being the one who introduced me to love. My bar is set high because of you and I wouldn't have it any other way! Rod Lipscomb, thank you sir for your friendship. We're doing it Lip!

My Clark Atlanta University Brothers and Atlanta family, Dave Morrision, Rod Hughes, Rahman Kafele, Anthony Smoak, Kibwe and Katrina Stanfield, Alex Casapu, Holland Turner, Demarcus Irons and Merertu Mulugeta(you inspire me, and I love you for that). My time in Atlanta saw me grow from a boy to a man and you all had something to do with that!

You can't survive in the city of Los Angeles as long as I have without having a second family to rely on. If it weren't for my family in Southern California I would have lost it a long time ago.

Omar Dorsey. Man, what can I say? We've been through a whole lot together. The mark of a true friendship is to be there for each other through the good times and bad. I never would have thought the first day on Drumline that I'd meet a best friend that I'd have for life. You were one of the first to believe in me man and I do not take that lightly. Watching your journey through manhood has been more exciting and inspiring than watching your journey career wise and that's saying a lot! Thank you for being there for me during my successes, failures, hearts breaks, anxiety attacks, everything. Let's take over the world only like Gingles and Dorsey can! Love you brother!

Shay Roundtree. Without your encouragement this book wouldn't exist. I tell people "Shay is a tough nut to crack but once he lets you in, he probably has the biggest heart of anyone I know." And that's true, man. You are a fearless friend and I love you for that. You're always pushing me to be better and that's never overlooked. You are talented in a number of areas but being the true definition of a human being is what you're best at.

Eugene Byrd. What can I say, you are the brother I never had. Whether it is being steaming mad at you cause you beat me in a video game or relying on your conversations to get me through whatever it is I'm facing, good or bad. Man, I thank you for your trust and supporting whatever crazy vision I share with you. You too are a fearless friend and I love you for that brother! It's dope seeing you grow as a person and an artist.

Selena Schoups. I know I'll never be alone in this world as long as you're in my life. One of my oldest friends here in LA, I appreciate you so much. Your kindness, generosity, loyalty and love have added light to my life. We pretty much came in this game together and we're going to reach our potential together too. I'm so proud of you. Love you mama!

Cathy Doe. My big sis. Words cannot explain how much you mean to me. Your support, advice and friendship has pulled me out of so many dark places that I can't even keep count anymore! Thank you for allowing me to be myself and removing the fear of judgment in our talks. That removal of fear has carried over into my creative life and I must thank you for that. Love you much!

Michael Velasquez. If one were to look up the word friend in a dictionary it would simply be a picture of you in one of your hilarious look away from the camera poses. We've been through the trenches together creatively and in life. It was truly a blessing the day we met. I can always count on you to be there. I can always count on you to support me through any creative journey. I want to create my best work with you in my corner, I need you Man! You are one of the coolest people to ever walk this planet and I consider it an honor to have you in my life. Thank you for everything including this awesome book cover! Love you man!

My beach crew! All of you guys are awesome! I don't know if you guys are aware of how much happiness you all bring to my life by just existing! Nancy, Brad, Leonard, Ted, Molly, Brittany, Sam, Roger and Naya. Ethan Lader, my oldest friend here in Los Angeles, you have been an amazing friend. I always look forward to your brutally honest yet love-filled conversations. I love the fact that we can talk about anything, anytime and any place. You inspire me man. Love you brother!

Music has always had an influence on me. I'd like to thank these artist for being the soundtrack to my life: Tupac Shakur, Marvin Gaye, Common, Outkast, The Red Hot Chili Peppers, Jimi Hendrix, Brian Wilson, Kurt Cobain, Kendrick Lamar, Scarface (thank you for always being one call away), John Williams, Jerry Goldsmith, Pharrell Williams, Prince, Michael Jackson and Kanye West.

There are so many people out there that I need to thank. Liz Edwards, Marlon Hunter, Natasha Ward, Jahmel Holden, Sean Blakemore, Dorian and Simone Missick, Sam Cook (one of the realest people I've ever met), Veronica Nichols (Ladybug!), Chloe Weaver, Shayla Rae Williams, Chezik Tsunoda, Yroko Marie Drevon, Evita Castorena, Khadeeja Abdul-Jabbar, Shannon Young, Kristy Garcia, Gigi Young, Andrea Reese(Listen… you're amazing, never forget that because I know I won't), Julius Ritter(my Burbank and writing brother!), Josh Leon, Sean Poolman, Tim Perrine (know that you and I will work together for ever!), The honorable Dick Gregory (Thank you to you and your family), Nicholas Buggs, Brad Schiefelbein, Major Latimer, Al Thompson, Ryan and Ace Young, Will and Tamica Fuller family, Mrs. Dee and Skip Johnson, Naoko and Kade Velasquez, Conisha, Olivia and Olympia Dorsey, "Big Game" James Lesure, The big homie Marcellus Wiley(Weekend Warriors unite! Louis and Eddie!), Lina Loi (My lovely and brilliant song writing partner. Let's continue to create beautiful music together), Megan Roundtree, Antonia Acevedob (thanks for always encouraging me to write and share,) Annelise Schoups, Duke Pryor, Lori Johnson and family (Love you Lady) Meagan Tandy, Sia Nyorkor, B'Randy Brooks, Carlos Davis (thanks for the publishing advice), Lauren Smith (my dear friend), Shana Edwards, LaToy Brooks, Lila DoVan(the purest soul I know), and Rhonda Simmons.

My last acknowledgement goes to Anthony 'TJ' Lasley. It's been 19 years since God called you home. Losing you was the first traumatic experience I ever went through in life and was the first time I tried on a mask to conceal the pain I was experiencing. I often questioned God why he called you home so early. It took me years to have closure with the situation. Every time I went back home to Indianapolis for the first fourteen years I drove past your house, hoping to relive a memory… a memory of us playing ball, a memory of us discovering music, a memory of a friendship. I often wished I'd catch your parents outside watering the lawn, washing their car or just walking in from a hard day at work just to have an excuse to stop the car, get out and speak. It never happened. I never had the courage to walk up to that door again and ring their bell. It hurts too much. I know once I do and that door opens with that familiar smell of your house hitting my nose I'll lose it. I know I said I had closure earlier, but I don't. We shared dreams and visions of moving to Los Angeles together. We were going to conquer the world. We talked about this in 1992. I'm here now and you're here in spirit, so we still did it man. Every success I have, you have. Every cool thing I experience, you experience.

I love you man, rest in heaven.

I know I'm leaving out some people. Please charge it to my mind and not my heart. I love you all dearly. Thank you all for being you!

Terry Gingles Jr.

www.ingramcontent.com/pod-product-compliance
Lightning Source LLC
LaVergne TN
LVHW091224080426
835509LV00009B/1160